Glossary

ceremony – a special event

continent – a large area of land that is split into different countries

evil – very bad

oil lamp – a lamp which burns oil to make light

powder – a dry substance made of many small bits

powerful – describes someone who is control and can do lots of things

priest – someone who works in a mandir

shrine – a special place to pray. It might have a picture or a small statue to remind people who they are praying to.

worship – pray or do something special to show that you think a god is important

Index

Answers:

1: Ganesha; 2: Ring a bell; 3: Seven; 4: Five days; 5: Holi; 6: India

Teaching notes:

Children who are reading Bookband Gold or above should be able to enjoy this book with some independence. Other children will need more support.

Before you share the book:

- Are any of the children in your class Hindus? Can they tell you about their experiences and understanding?
- Talk together about the religions of other children. What is the same/what is different from Hindu children's experiences?

While you share the book:

- Help children to read some of the more unfamiliar words and concepts.

- Talk about the questions. Encourage children of different faiths and no faith to share their own answers.
- Talk about the pictures. Help children to identify who or what the captions refer to: Where are the statues (p10)? Who is the priest (p11)? Where is the stone (p15)? Where are the lamps (p16)? Although the vocabulary should be familiar, the context may not be.

After you have shared the book:

- Find out more about other Hindu gods and goddesses. What do people pray to them about?
- Arrange to take the children to visit a mandir. Ask them to look for things mentioned or shown in the book.
- Work through the free activity sheets from our Teacher Zone at www.hachettechildrens.co.uk

Series Contents Lists

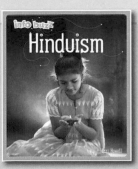

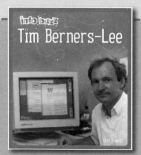

FRANKLIN WATTS

Fierce Fighters
GLADIATORS AND ROMAN SOLDIERS

Charlotte Guillain

Raintree

Raintree is an imprint of Capstone Global Library Limited,
a company incorporated in England and Wales having its
registered office at 7 Pilgrim Street, London, EC4V 6LB
– Registered company number: 6695582

Text © Capstone Global Library Limited 2010
First published in hardback in 2010
The moral rights of the proprietor have been asserted.

Edited by Rebecca Rissman, Nancy Dickmann, and
Catherine Veitch
Designed by Joanna Hinton-Malivoire
Picture research by Tracy Cummins
Original illlustrations © Capstone Global Library 2010
Original illustrations by Miracle Studios
Production by Victoria Fitzgerald
Originated by Capstone Global Library
Printed and bound in China by Leo Paper Products

ISBN 978 1 406 21611 0
14 13 12 11 10
10 9 8 7 6 5 4 3 2 1

British Library Cataloguing in Publication Data
Guillain, Charlotte.
Gladiators and Roman soldiers. -- (Fierce fighters)
355.1'0937-dc22

Acknowledgements
We would like to thank the following for permission to
reproduce photographs: akg-images pp. **22** (Electa),
26; Alamy pp. **11** (© Jeff Morgan heritage), **14** (©
Jeff Morgan heritage), **20** (© The Print Collector);
Art Resource, NY p. **24** (© The Trustees of The British
Museum); Corbis pp. **9** (© Sandro Vannini), **16**
(© Hoberman Collection); Getty Images p. **12** (AFP/
FILIPPO MONTEFORTE); Heinemann Raintree pp. **28
top** (Karon Dubke), **28 bottom** (Karon Dubke), **29**
(Karon Dubke); Photolibrary p. **23** (The Print Collector);
Shutterstock pp. **6** (© Chen Ping Hung), **13** (© Regien
Paassen), **17** (© David Harding), **18** (© Petronilo G.
Dangoy Jr.), **27**(© Forum Romanum); The Art Archive
p. **25** (Musée Archéologique Naples / Gianni Dagli Orti).

Front cover illustration of a Roman battle reproduced
with permission of Miracle Studios.

The publishers would like to thank Jane Penrose for her
assistance in the preparation of this book.

Every effort has been made to contact copyright holders
of material reproduced in this book. Any omissions will
be rectified in subsequent printings if notice is given to
the publishers.

All the internet addresses (URLs) given in this book were
valid at the time of going to press. However, due to the
dynamic nature of the Internet, some addresses may have
changed or ceased to exist since publication. While the
author and publishers regret any inconvenience this may
cause readers, no responsibility for any such changes can
be accepted by either the author or the publishers.

Some words are shown in bold, **like this**. You can find
out what they mean by looking in the glossary.

Contents

Roaring Romans

Place: Village in Britain

Date: AD 43

4

Rows of soldiers are marching towards a village. Arrows and **spears** fly through the air. The villagers fought hard but they have lost.

The Roman army has won another battle.

Roman timeline

27 BC	Start of the Roman Empire
AD 43	Romans invade Britain
AD 476	Western Roman Empire ends
1600s	People from Europe start to settle in North America
2000s	You are reading this book

Who were the Romans?

The Romans ruled a huge area of land called an **empire**. First they built the city of Rome. Then Roman soldiers moved through Europe and North Africa, winning war after war.

The Roman Empire

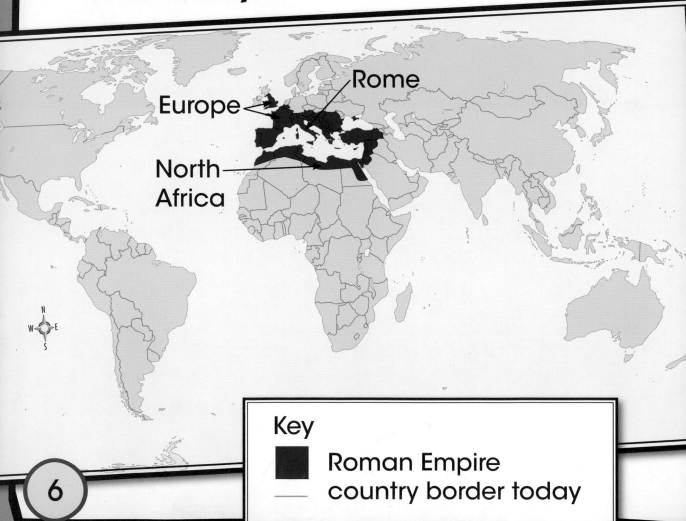

Rome

Europe

North Africa

Key

■ Roman Empire

— country border today

DID YOU KNOW?

Romans loved fighting.
They even watched fighters
killing each other for fun.

Roman soldiers

Roman soldiers were hard to beat. They were strong and fit. They could build roads and bridges. This meant they could march anywhere.

DID YOU KNOW?
Romans had **slaves** to break up stones for building roads.

9

A Roman soldier's training was tough.
They had to go on long marches,
as well as doing lots of swimming.
They practised fighting with a heavy
wooden sword to make them strong.

onager

Romans used an
onager to fire heavy
stones at their enemy.
The stones could
smash down walls.

Roman weapons

Roman soldiers wore heavy metal helmets and **armour**. They carried a short sword and **dagger** in their belts. Romans used their shields to stop enemy weapons hurting them.

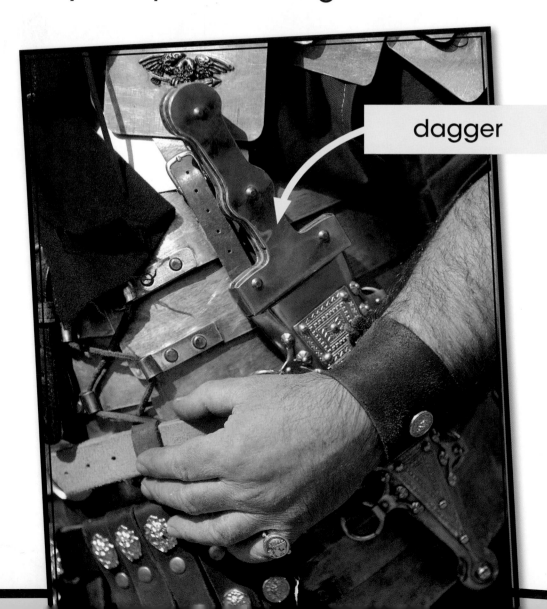

dagger

shield

In battle, Roman soldiers threw **spears** called **pila** at their enemies. Sometimes the pila got stuck in enemy shields. This made it hard for the enemy to use the shields. Then the Roman soldiers attacked with swords.

DID YOU KNOW?

When the enemy attacked, Roman soldiers stood close together in rows. They held up their shields so the enemy could not hurt them.

pila

15

Great general

Julius Caesar was a great Roman **general**. He led his army into northern France and took the land there for the Roman **Empire**. The soldiers helped Caesar beat his enemies and become leader of all the Roman Empire.

coin showing Julius Caesar

DID YOU KNOW?

Caesar was the first Roman general to attack Britain.

Gruesome Gladiators

Romans liked to go to a large arena called a **stadium** to see people fight each other and animals. These fighters were called **gladiators**. The crowd wanted to see the gladiators die fighting.

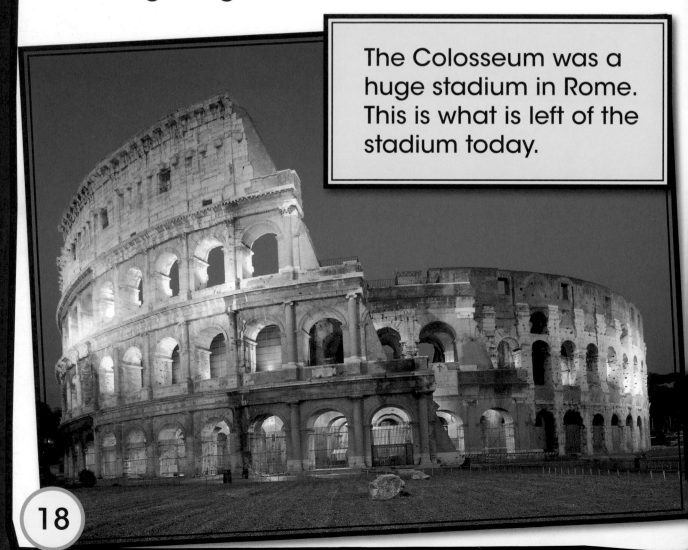

The Colosseum was a huge stadium in Rome. This is what is left of the stadium today.

gladiators

DID YOU KNOW?

Romans also enjoyed watching lions and crocodiles eat people.

Gladiators were **slaves** or prisoners who were made to fight. Some trained at gladiator schools. Fights usually ended when one gladiator died. A hurt gladiator might get to live if the crowd cheered enough.

DID YOU KNOW?

Some gladiators became famous and had many supporters, like today's sports stars.

Gladiator weapons

Gladiators fought each other with different weapons. Some gladiators fought with a net, a **dagger**, and a big fork called a **trident**. Others had to fight wearing a helmet with no eyeholes. They could not see where they were going!

dagger

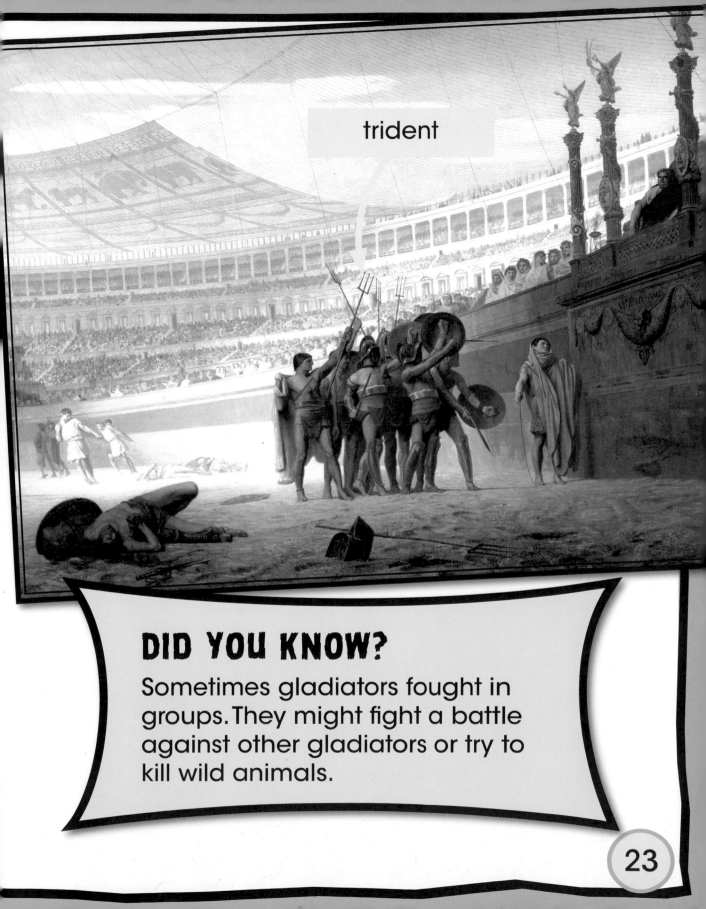

trident

DID YOU KNOW?

Sometimes gladiators fought in groups. They might fight a battle against other gladiators or try to kill wild animals.

Roman women

Women could not join the army but some **gladiators** were women. Women took part in **chariot** races and fought each other and wild animals.

This carving shows female gladiators.

DID YOU KNOW?

Roman girls were very young when they got married. Some were only 14 years old.

The end of the Romans

The main Roman **Empire** lasted for about 500 years. Then weak Roman leaders started to fight each other. The Romans lost control of the land the army had won. The Western Empire was finished.

You can still see the **ruins** of Roman buildings in Rome today.

Roman activity

Different sections of the Roman army had a banner or **standard**. One soldier carried the standard at the front as they marched.

Make your own standard

You will need:
- a long cardboard tube
- three small paper plates
- card
- gold and silver paper
- red crepe paper
- scissors
- pencil
- PVA glue

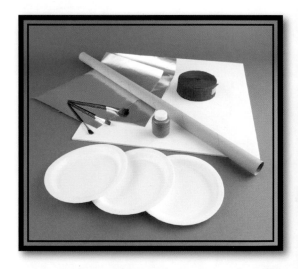

1. Cut out a rectangle of card and cover it with gold paper. Stick this card at the top of the tube.

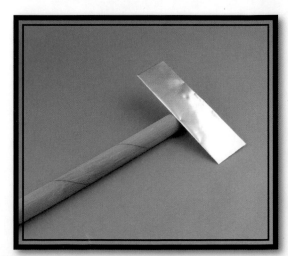

2. Cut out two long strips of red crepe paper and stick them to either end of the rectangle.

3. Cover the paper plates with silver paper and stick them on the tube, under the gold rectangle.

4. Cover another piece of card with silver paper. Draw around your hand on the card. Cut the hand shape out and stick it at the top of your standard.

You are ready to march into battle!

Glossary

armour covering made of metal or leather to protect a soldier

chariot open carriage with two wheels pulled by horses

dagger small sword

empire large area ruled by a king or emperor

general an important army officer

gladiator person trained to fight to entertain the public

pila long, light spears used as weapons by Roman soldiers

slaves people who were owned by other people and had to work for no pay

spear weapon with sharp point on a long pole

stadium sports ground surrounded on all sides by rows of seats

standard banner carried into battle

trident large fork used by gladiators as a weapon

Find out more

Books

Gladiators, Michael Martin
(Capstone Edge Books, 2007)

Staying Alive in Ancient Rome,
Brenda and Brian Williams (Raintree Fusion, 2008)

Time Travel Guide: Ancient Rome,
John Malam (Heinemann/Raintree, 2008)

Websites

www.historyforkids.org/learn/romans/
This website has lots of information about the ancient Romans.

www.pbs.org/empires/romans
This website has information about the Roman Empire, including maps and a timeline.

Places to visit

Hadrian's Wall, Northumberland
www.nationaltrail.co.uk/hadrianswall/

Fishbourne Roman Palace, Sussex
www.sussexpast.co.uk/property/site.php?site_id=11

Roman Baths, Bath
www.romanbaths.co.uk

The British Museum, London
www.britishmuseum.org/

Find out

What food did Romans like to eat?